ONEY FARM • OYSTER FARM • ROOFTOP GA
FOOD FOREST • ROOM FARM • OYSTER FARM
ISH FARM • FO ARM • MUSHROOM FARM • OYST
DOBA • FISH FARM • FOOD FOREST • HONEY FARM • MUSHROOM FA OYST
AR GARDEN • DOBA • FISH FARM • FOOD FOREST • HONEY FARM • MUSHROOM F
SPHERE • CIRCULAR GARDEN • DOBA • FISH FARM • FOOD FOREST • HONEY FAR
ICAL FARM • BIOSPHERE • CIRCULAR GARDEN • DOBA • FISH FARM • FOOD FO
ARM • VERTICAL FARM • BIOSPHERE • CIRCULAR GARDEN • DOBA • FISH FARM
TERRACE FARM • VERTICAL FARM • BIOSPHERE • CIRCULAR GARDEN • DOBA
SALT FARM • TERRACE FARM • VERTICAL FARM • BIOSPHERE • CIRCULAR GA
TOP GARDEN • SALT FARM • TERRACE FARM • VERTICAL FARM • BIOSPHERE • C
RM • ROOFTOP GARDEN • SALT FARM • TERRACE FARM • VERTICAL FARM • BIO
OYSTER FARM • ROOFTOP GARDEN • SALT FARM • TERRACE FARM • VERTICAL
OM FARM • OYSTER FARM • ROOFTOP GARDEN • SALT FARM • TERRACE FARM •
MUSHROOM FARM • OYSTER FARM • ROOFTOP GARDEN • SALT FARM • TERRAC
HONEY FARM • MUSHROOM FARM • OYSTER FARM • ROOFTOP GARDEN • SALT FA
FOOD FOREST • HONEY FARM • MUSHROOM FARM • OYSTER FARM • ROOFTOP GA
ISH FARM • FOOD FOREST • HONEY FARM • MUSHROOM FARM • OYSTER FARM •
DOBA • FISH FARM • FOOD FOREST • HONEY FARM • MUSHROOM FARM • OYST
AR GARDEN • DOBA • FISH FARM • FOOD FOREST • HONEY FARM • MUSHROOM F
SPHERE • CIRCULAR GARDEN • DOBA • FISH FARM • FOOD FOREST • HONEY FAR
ICAL FARM • BIOSPHERE • CIRCULAR GARDEN • DOBA • FISH FARM • FOOD FO
ARM • VERTICAL FARM • BIOSPHERE • CIRCULAR GARDEN • DOBA • FISH FAR
TERRACE FARM • VERTICAL FARM • BIOSPHERE • CIRC
SALT FARM • TERRACE FARM • VERTICAL FARM • BIO

AL FARM • BIOSPHERE • CIRCULAR GARDEN • DOBA • FISH FARM • FOOD FORE
FARM • VERTICAL FARM • BIOSPHERE • CIRCULAR GARDEN • DOBA • FISH FA
M • TERRACE FARM • VERTICAL FARM • BIOSPHERE • CIRCULAR GARDEN • DOB
• SALT FARM • TERRACE FARM • VERTICAL FARM • BIOSPHERE • CIRCULAR GA
OP GARDEN • SALT FARM • TERRACE FARM • VERTICAL FARM • BIOSPHERE • C
ER FARM • ROOFTOP GARDEN • SALT FARM • TERRACE FARM • VERTICAL FARM
OOM FARM • OYSTER FARM • ROOFTOP GARDEN • SALT FARM • TERRACE FARM •
M • MUSHROOM FARM • OYSTER FARM • ROOFTOP GARDEN • SALT FARM • TER
• HONEY FARM • MUSHROOM FARM • OYSTER FARM • ROOFTOP GARDEN • SALT
FOOD FOREST • HONEY FARM • MUSHROOM FARM • OYSTER FARM • ROOFTOP GA
ISH FARM • FOOD FOREST • HONEY FARM • MUSHROOM FARM • OYSTER FARM •
DOBA • FISH FARM • FOOD FOREST • HONEY FARM • MUSHROOM FARM • OYST
R GARDEN • DOBA • FISH FARM • FOOD FOREST • HONEY FARM • MUSHROOM FA
• CIRCULAR GARDEN • DOBA • FISH FARM • FOOD FOREST • HONEY FARM • M
IOSPHERE • CIRCULAR GARDEN • DOBA • FISH FARM • FOOD FOREST • HONEY F
AL FARM • BIOSPHERE • CIRCULAR GARDEN • DOBA • FISH FARM • FOOD FORE
FARM • VERTICAL FARM • BIOSPHERE • CIRCULAR GARDEN • DOBA • FISH FA
M • TERRACE FARM • VERTICAL FARM • BIOSPHERE • CIRCULAR GARDEN • DOB
• SALT FARM • TERRACE FARM • VERTICAL FARM • BIOSPHERE • CIRCULAR GA
OP GARDEN • SALT FARM • TERRACE FARM • VERTICAL FARM • BIOSPHERE • C
ER FARM • ROOFTOP GARDEN • SALT FARM • TERRACE FARM • VERTICAL FARM
OOM FARM • OYSTER FARM • ROOFTOP GARDEN • SALT FARM • TERRACE FARM •
M • MUSHROOM FARM • OYSTER FARM • ROOFTOP GARDEN • SALT FARM • TER
• HONEY FARM • MUSHROOM FARM • OYSTER FARM • ROOFTOP GARDEN • SALT
FOOD FOREST • HONEY FARM • MUSHROOM FARM • OYSTER FARM • ROOFTOP GA

FOOD FOR THE FUTURE

Sustainable Farms Around the World

To my daughter Zoe, who is creating wind-farm-based aquaculture systems — MIA WENJEN

To my abuelo and his kidney bean farm in Mexico — ROBERT SAE-HENG

Barefoot Books would like to thank the following people for their help in the creation of this book:

María-Verónica A. Barnes, Director of Diversity Education, Lexington Montessori School

Dr. John Gerber, Professor of Sustainable Food & Farming, University of Massachusetts

Emily Golightly, Media Coordinator / Librarian, Newport Elementary School

---

Barefoot Books
23 Bradford Street, 2nd Floor
Concord, MA 01742

Barefoot Books
29/30 Fitzroy Square
London, W1T 6LQ

Text copyright © 2023 by Mia Wenjen
Illustrations copyright © 2023 by Robert Sae-Heng
The moral rights of Mia Wenjen and Robert Sae-Heng
have been asserted

First published in the United States of America
by Barefoot Books, Inc and in Great Britain by
Barefoot Books, Ltd in 2023
All rights reserved

Graphic design by Elizabeth Jayasekera, Barefoot Books
Edited and art directed by Lisa Rosinsky, Barefoot Books

Reproduction by Bright Arts, Hong Kong
Printed in Malaysia

This book was typeset in Beautiful Freak, Filson Soft,
Kindness Matters and Metallophile Sp8
The illustrations were created using digital brushes

Hardback ISBN 978-1-64686-839-1
Paperback ISBN 978-1-64686-840-7
E-book ISBN 978-1-64686-864-3

British Cataloguing-in-Publication Data: a catalogue record
for this book is available from the British Library

Library of Congress Cataloging-in-Publication Data
is available under LCCN 2022053305

1 3 5 7 9 8 6 4 2

FOOD FOR THE FUTURE

Sustainable Farms Around the World

words by **MIA WENJEN**   art by **ROBERT SAE-HENG**

Barefoot Books

Step inside a story

Can we feed the world without pollution?
Sustainable farms are one solution.

We can go back to old ways or try something new.
Let's take care of our Earth — for me and for you!

sustainable: living or working in a way that protects people and the planet

SALT FARM (USA)

Salt from Kaua`i* preserves ancient ways.
Seawater dries in the hot sun for days.

*kuh-WAI-ee

preserves: keeps
something going

FOOD FOREST (Kenya)

In Nairobi*, edible food forests unveil
A feast of guavas, bananas and kale.

*nai-ROH-bee

edible: something that is safe to eat

Bees live in a hive with a large family brood,
Working together to make their own food.

brood: a group of
babies in a family

MUSHROOM FARM (Mexico)

compost: organic waste like leaves and rotting food that can be mixed with soil to help plants grow

Mushrooms are able to grow in the dark,
Sprouting from beds of compost or bark.

ROOFTOP GARDEN (USA)

This rooftop garden, a new landmark,
Grows food for fans at Fenway Park.

landmark: something you can easily recognize from far away or that helps people figure out where they are

dam: something that blocks water in a river or makes it flow in a new direction, such as a pile of logs (log jam)

Enawenê-Nawê* people build a log jam
With handwoven fish traps placed in the dam.

*en-ah-wen-EH nah-WEH

VERTICAL FARM (Singapore)

Tree-shaped gardens in giant towers
Collect rainwater and make solar power.

solar power: electricity made from sunlight

TERRACE FARM (Chile)

Potatoes and quinoa* grow on the hillside,
Where gardens in terraces hold back landslides.

*KEEN-wah

terrace: steps built into a hillside to create more room for growing plants and keep water from flowing away downhill

Nemo's Garden grows deep in the ocean,
Where greenhouse pods sway with gentle motion.

greenhouse pods: clear plastic containers for growing plants

Farmers hatch oysters in nurseries,
Then grow them in cages that float at sea.

nursery: a place where young creatures are cared for

CIRCULAR GARDEN (Senegal)

Thirsty gardens designed for the heat
Grow where Sahara and savanna meet.

Sahara: the desert that stretches across most of north Africa

savanna: a grassy area of land without many trees

DOBA (India)

Dobas are pits for rainfall collection,
With grasses and plants for soil protection.

soil protection: using plants to hold dirt in place against **erosion** (getting washed away by rain and wind)

Our world is changing and farming must too,
With Indigenous ways and modern breakthroughs.

Let's grow food together on land and at sea.
Looking after our Earth will create harmony.

breakthrough: an important discovery or invention

WHAT IS SUSTAINABLE FARMING?

Food for Now, Food for Later

Sustainable farming means producing enough food to feed people now while also making sure there will be enough for people to eat in the future. These farms grow food without using too much energy, water or harmful chemicals, and without harming the **habitats** (homes) of animals who live nearby. Some types of sustainable farms have been around for thousands of years, while others are modern inventions. Sustainable farms aim to take care of everyone: the farmer, the community and the Earth.

What Is Food Justice?

The big idea behind **food justice** is that everyone deserves healthy, affordable food to eat. About one-tenth of the world, or more than 600 million people, suffer from **food insecurity**, which means that they don't have enough food. There can be many reasons why. It may be hard for people to get jobs or live near affordable grocery stores. **Climate change** (the warming of our planet caused by human activity) can make it difficult for people to grow their own food. Also, when big companies own enormous farms, that makes it hard for small farms and workers to earn enough money to stay in business.

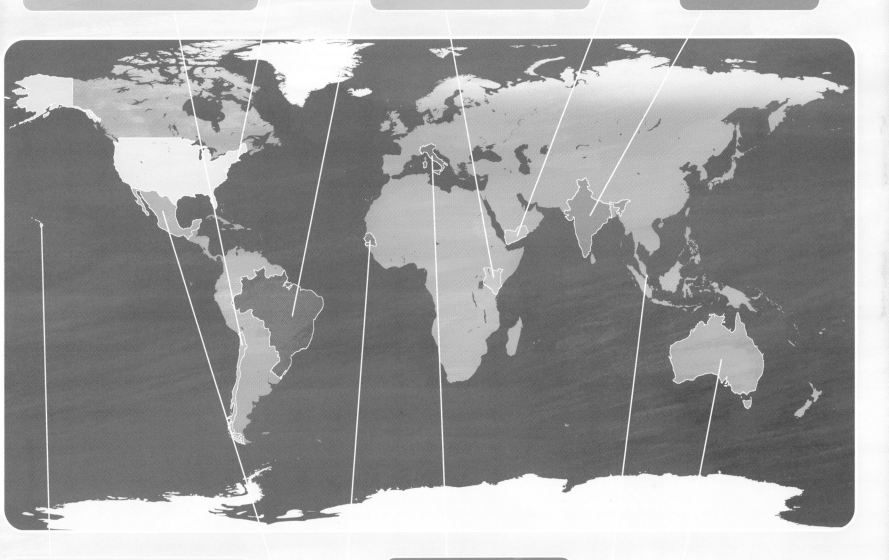

ROOFTOP GARDEN (Boston, USA)

FISH FARM (Brazil)

HONEY FARM (Yemen)

TERRACE FARM (Chile)

FOOD FOREST (Kenya)

DOBA (India)

SALT FARM (Hawai'i USA)

BIOSPHERE (Italy)

MUSHROOM FARM (Mexico)

VERTICAL FARM (Singapore)

CIRCULAR GARDEN (Senegal)

OYSTER FARM (Australia)

Which of these farms is closest to where you live? Which would you most like to visit someday?

SALT FARM (USA)

- **Where does it come from?** In ancient Hawai'i, `alaea (ah-LAI-ah) salt was created when ocean water mixed with red clay from the island's rivers and became trapped in rocks near the seashore. When the water dried, it left behind salt.

- **How does it work?** Native Hawaiians created shallow clay ponds to harvest more `alaea salt. Each summer, families in Kaua`i (kuh-WAI-ee) continue this tradition. First, saltwater from underground wells is moved to shallow pools called wai kū (wai koo), shaped from Kaua`i's red earth. As the water **evaporates**, turning from liquid into gas, salt crystals form. These crystals are transferred to a basket and rinsed with fresh water. The salt dries for six to eight weeks and then is ready to be used. A tiny amount of clay gathered from the mountains nearby is mixed with the salt to make it red.

- **Why is it sustainable?** `Alaea salt is harvested using only natural elements: sunshine, red clay soil and lava stones to shape the salt beds. Increased rain and rising sea levels caused by climate change threaten the salt beds in Kaua`i.

- **Did you know?** `Alaea salt is used for cooking, as medicine and in rituals to bless homes, canoes, temples and tools.

FOOD FOREST (Kenya)

- **Where does it come from?** Many Kenyans traditionally raised animals for food but climate change has caused less rain to fall. This means not enough food and water for animals and for people. Some people now plant food forests instead of raising animals as a way to grow enough food for their communities.

- **How does it work?** A food forest looks like the edge of a forest but is planted with fruit and nut trees, berry bushes and edible plants, so that every level of the forest provides food. The Kenyan food forests are planted with Indigenous fruit trees such as African oak, whose nutritious and high-protein seeds can be ground and used for flour.

- **Why is it sustainable?** A food forest is **self-maintaining** which means that people don't need to weed, fertilize or compost the plants.

- **Did you know?** Food forests in Kenya help to bring trees and forests back to land that has been damaged by **erosion** (soil washing away) and **drought** (lack of rain).

HONEY FARM (Yemen)

- **Where does it come from?** Farmers over 9,000 years ago tamed the honey bee so they could gather honey and wax for food and medicine. Today, there are honey farms in nearly every country in the world!

- **How does it work?** In the wild, honey bees live in forests, eat nectar from nearby plants and build their hives inside trees using wax honeycomb. On honey farms, beekeepers give their bees homes near flowering plants, medicine if they get ill and even new **queen bees** (mother bees) if the hives need them. Yemen honey farmers move their beehives in search of flowering wild sidr (SEE-der) trees, an ancient evergreen tree, but these are harder and harder to find because of drought caused by climate change and war.

- **Why is it sustainable?** Honey is one of the most sustainable foods on earth, because all you need to produce it are bees and flowers! Bees are also good for the environment because they **pollinate** plants (help them make seeds) as they collect nectar.

- **Did you know?** There are more than 20,000 different types of bees in the world but only one kind makes enough honey for harvesting — honey bees.

MUSHROOM FARM (Mexico)

- **Where does it come from?** Mushrooms are grown all over the world. They are easy and cheap to grow and can adapt to many different environments. Since they are a good source of protein, they can be a vegetarian or vegan alternative to meat.

- **How does it work?** Mushrooms don't need energy from the sun, so they can grow in the dark! They grow by breaking down compost. Some can be grown on logs, but the mushrooms often found in grocery stores, such as button, cremini and portobello, are grown in mushroom houses like the one shown in this book.

- **Why is it sustainable?** Mushrooms use compost for their food, helping use up waste. And they don't require anything else to grow, which makes them one of the most sustainable crops. Farmers can also get as many as eight harvests in a single year!

- **Did you know?** Mexico's most famous mushroom, the huitlacoche (weet-luh-KOH-cheh), grows on corn! When a fungus called *Ustilago maydis* infects corn, it turns the kernels into blue-black mushrooms that taste smoky and delicious. Huitlacoches make great quesadilla fillings!

ROOFTOP GARDEN (USA)

- **Where does it come from?** Boston's baseball team, the Red Sox, created Fenway Farms on an empty roof at Fenway Park in 2015.

- **How does it work?** The rooftop garden at Fenway Park now grows over 4,000 pounds (1,814 kg) of food each baseball season. Fenway Farms serves the **produce** (fruit and vegetables) in the restaurants at Fenway Park and also uses it to teach young people about sustainability and healthy food choices.

- **Why is it sustainable?** The Red Sox have installed a smaller copy of their rooftop garden at the Boston Children's Museum where you can learn about sustainability and the life cycle of plants. Extra produce is given to animals at the museum and donated to a local nonprofit group.

- **Did you know?** Other baseball teams such as the San Diego Padres, San Francisco Giants, New York Yankees and Colorado Rockies have also built similar rooftop gardens at their stadiums so people can learn about healthy food and sustainable farming.

FISH FARM (Brazil)

- **Where does it come from?** The Indigenous Enawenê-Nawê (en-ah-wen-EH nah-WEH) tribe lives in a tropical forest near the Jurena River in western Brazil. They celebrate an annual cycle of rituals to live sustainably off the land, which include fish camps, music and dance.

- **How does it work?** During the wet season, men and boys go on a two-month fish camp. They build dams when fish swim up the river, with cone-shaped traps in the dams that catch the fish as they return downstream. After camp is over, the dam is destroyed so the fish can swim upriver to **spawn** (reproduce).

- **Why is it sustainable?** The Enawenê-Nawê use the natural life cycle of fish and the river itself to create a sustainable fish farm. Many of the fish they catch cannot be raised on human-made farms. The tribe's sustainable way of life is threatened by **deforestation** (when people cut down trees), water pollution and construction of commercial dams.

- **Did you know?** When the men and boys return from their fish camp, they perform a ceremony called Yãkwa (YAK-wah), where the food is presented to the spirit world.

VERTICAL FARM (Singapore)

- **Where does it come from?** Singapore is home to many vertical farms and gardens, such as Supertree Grove (shown in this book) and an incredible skyscraper greenhouse called Sky Greens.

- **How does it work?** Supertree Grove is a garden that generates solar energy and collects rainwater to grow more than 200 species of plants and flowers. Sky Greens is a farm made from rotating towers that grow Asian leafy vegetables like nai bai, xiao bai cai (shyau bai tsai) and Chinese cabbage.

- **Why is it sustainable?** Supertree Grove's system absorbs and disperses heat, replacing the need for a conventional air-conditioning system. Sky Greens' rotating towers do not use electricity, only gravity and a pulley system with water that is recycled and used to water the plants.

- **Did you know?** Singapore buys most of its food from other countries, which can be very expensive. Sky Greens was founded in 2009 to help the country grow more of its own food. Supertree Grove even has a restaurant at the top of the tallest tree!

TERRACE FARM (Chile)

- **Where does it come from?** Historians believe that terrace farming in Chile began as early as 2400 BCE, before the Inka civilization! The Atacameño (ah-tah-kah-MEN-yo) and Quechua (KETCH-wah) Indigenous people have farmed this way for thousands of years. In fact, terrace farming has been used for centuries all around the world.

- **How does it work?** Terrace farms are a series of steps built into the side of a mountain. Because the thin soil at the top is not good for planting, **fertile soil** (dirt that can nourish plants) is brought up from the valley below to fill each terraced plot. Water flows between each terrace in a slow and winding way so it is absorbed in the earth instead of running off. Terrace farms in Chile grow corn, quinoa (KEEN-wah), potatoes, garlic, apricots, apples, as well as other Andean vegetables such as caldas, añu, oca and ullucu.

- **Why is it sustainable?** There is very little water in northern Chile and there is not much fertile land high up in the mountains. Terrace farming makes the most of small amounts of water and nourishing soil.

- **Did you know?** Every village with a terrace farm has a "water official" to make sure water is shared fairly. Each land plot is passed down within a family. The farm grows enough food for the family to eat as well as extra to sell.

BIOSPHERE (Italy)

- **Where does it come from?** Sergio Gamberini, a scuba gear manufacturer, came up with the idea of an underwater greenhouse. He grew basil in a miniature version of the biosphere and noticed that it grew twice as fast as usual.

- **How does it work?** Nemo's Garden is one example of a **biosphere** — an independent bubble of life. It is an underwater garden made up of clear plastic pods filled with air and chained to the seafloor off the coast of Italy. Crops in Nemo's Garden are protected from extreme heat, cold and insect pests. The biospheres can be adjusted to float at different heights below the water's surface depending on how much sunlight and warmth the crops need. In the pods, strawberries, lettuce and herbs such as basil, thyme, lemon balm and marjoram are grown using **hydroponics**, a system that grows plants using nutrient-enriched water instead of soil.

- **Why is it sustainable?** The water needed for plants in Nemo's Garden is created by removing salt from seawater, which turns it into fresh water. This is helpful if freshwater is unavailable or scarce.

- **Did you know?** Nemo's Garden is a place to test new ideas for areas where land-based farming is not possible, such as outer space.

OYSTER FARM (Australia)

- **Where does it come from?** Oyster farming is one of the oldest forms of **aquaculture** (farming in the water). Indigenous Australians enjoyed oysters for thousands of years before Europeans arrived.

- **How does it work?** Oyster farming begins when eggs are placed in a **hatchery**, an indoor tank with warm, moist air. The swimming **larvae**, or baby oysters, are moved to a storage tank where they begin to grow their shell. When the baby oysters are about ¼ inch (0.6 cm) in size, they are placed in bags in **estuaries** (where a river meets the ocean). Next, they are put in cages out at sea or directly on the sea floor until they are ready to harvest.

- **Why is it sustainable?** Oysters are a **zero-input crop**, which means they get everything they need to grow from the sun and their environment (the ocean) and do not need farmers to give them any other food or water.

- **Did you know?** Oysters filter water as they feed, removing harmful pollutants from the water. They absorb these materials with their shells or deposit them at the bottom of the ocean where they are not harmful.

CIRCULAR GARDEN (Senegal)

- **Where does it come from?** During the COVID-19 pandemic in 2020, Senegal shut its borders to slow the spread of the virus. Circular gardens called tolou keur (toh-looh KURR) were started to help rural areas produce their own food and medicine.

- **How does it work?** The circular design allows plant roots to grow inwards towards the middle, trapping liquids and bacteria. Farmers dig shallow pits called zai throughout the farm fields to trap rain. **Manure** (animal poop) fertilizes the plants and encourages termites to tunnel through the soil, adding air pockets that help plants grow. The gardens grow papayas, cashews, lemons and medicinal plants, as well as baobab and African mahogany trees.

- **Why is it sustainable?** The Sahel area in Africa, where the Sahara Desert and the green savanna meet, is severely affected by climate change. Drought and food insecurity are a constant worry. Senegal's circular gardens are a part of the effort to prevent the desert from taking over.

- **Did you know?** Circular gardens are part of the Green Wall project, which began in 2007. The goal of this project is to plant 4,970 miles (8,000 km) of trees across the middle of Africa, from Senegal to Djibouti (djuh-BOO-tee).

DOBA (India)

- **Where does it come from?** Water harvesting is an Indigenous practice of saving and storing water in the rainy season so it can be used in the drier months.

- **How does it work?** In India, there is a dry season and a wet season. Climate change has caused hotter temperatures and drought, which have made it difficult to grow food during the dry season. The government is teaching farmers how to gather water during the wet season using human-made pits called dobas, then store the water to use during the dry season. They grow vegetables, sugarcane, grains and fruit such as guava, lemon, jackfruit, mango and banana.

- **Why is it sustainable?** Farmers also grow plants and grasses on the edges of the dobas to prevent erosion. The government-run water harvesting education is also an example of food justice.

- **Did you know?** Because the dobas don't dry out, they can also be used to raise small fish which farmers and their families can eat.

AUTHOR'S NOTE

My interest in sustainable farming started thanks to my son's love of seafood, particularly raw oysters on the half-shell. A birthday dinner at an oyster farm restaurant led to a tour of the oyster farm, where we learned that some New England lobster farmers had switched to oyster farming in the wake of dropping prices and global warming.

The idea for this book came from our oyster farm experience combined with a photo of the circular farms in Senegal that I saw on social media. Both were such different ways of adapting to our changing world. It jogged my memory of the salt farms in Kaua`i we drove by while on vacation. Then my research started in earnest to find unusual sustainable farms all over the world.

Climate change affects us all, but it gives me hope that there are sustainable farms all over the world. Collectively, this is how we will find a way to feed our planet. Personally, I am inspired to start a food forest! I hope readers are inspired to try something too.

— **Mia Wenjen**

ILLUSTRATOR'S NOTE

I live and work in London, England, with my colossal cheese plant named Elvis. (A cheese plant has big green leaves with holes in them, like Swiss cheese — it's not a plant that grows cheese!) I love to travel and explore, documenting my experiences through drawing. I especially enjoy drawing quirky things with lots of personality, like seals and quaint chairs. I also like to create mini stories for the characters that appear in my research and drawings, imagining how they interact with their surroundings.

After researching each of the farms for this book, I first drew them in my sketchbook using pencils and then transferred these sketches to my iPad. I reflected a lot on my own experience growing up in a tiny village in Mexico where my sister and I helped and played on our grandfather's kidney bean farm.

— **Robert Sae-Heng**

Barefoot Books
step inside a story

At Barefoot Books, we celebrate art and story that opens the hearts and minds of children from all walks of life, focusing on themes that encourage independence of spirit, enthusiasm for learning and respect for the world's diversity. The welfare of our children is dependent on the welfare of the planet, so we source paper from sustainably managed forests and constantly strive to reduce our environmental impact. Playful, beautiful and created to last a lifetime, our products combine the best of the present with the best of the past to educate our children as the caretakers of tomorrow.

www.barefootbooks.com

MIA WENJEN

enjoys boxing, gardening and yoga. Because Japanese cucumbers are not available where she lives, she sprouted them from seed and convinced her boxing gym friends to grow them as well. She lives in Boston, USA, with her husband, three children and Golden Retriever. She blogs on parenting, education and children's books at *PragmaticMom.com* and runs the nonprofit Multicultural Children's Book Day.

ROBERT SAE-HENG

is an illustrator and artist living in London, UK, with his fantastically large cheese plant (also known as a monstera) named Elvis. He has Mexican and Thai origins, and spent his childhood on a tiny farm in Mexico. He first began using imagery to communicate because he spent his early years unable to hear. Robert now works with mixed media, combining hand-drawn elements with a digital finish.